HAL LEONARD

STEELPAN METHOD
EAGUE

To access audio visit:
www.halleonard.com/mylibrary

5914-8625-9633-2580

ISBN 978-1-4950-0672-2

HAL•LEONARD®
CORPORATION

7777 W. BLUEMOUND RD. P.O. BOX 13819 MILWAUKEE, WI 53213

In Australia Contact:
Hal Leonard Australia Pty. Ltd.
4 Lentara Court
Cheltenham, Victoria, 3192 Australia
Email: ausadmin@halleonard.com.au

Visit Hal Leonard Online at
www.halleonard.com

INTRODUCTION

This method book is geared towards the beginning student and will examine approaches to playing the steelpan.

The steelpan is the national instrument of Trinidad and Tobago and is generally referred to as the "pan"; though, outside of the Caribbean, it is mainly known by the name "steel drum." In its native country, the highest pitched pan is called the "tenor pan" or "lead pan"; however, since the range of the pan mimics the range of a soprano, it can also be called "soprano pan."

One who plays the steelpan is called a pannist (sometimes spelled "panist").

"Steelband" or "steel orchestra" are the terms used to describe an ensemble consisting of the different steelpan voices (e.g., soprano, double second, cello, bass, etc.).

While the pan has made significant advances in its relatively short history, a completely standardized and accepted placement of notes is still not firmly established (though there are some note layouts which are more common than others).

The great steelpan innovator, Anthony "Tony" Williams, created a soprano pan (called the "Spider Web") with a note pattern based on the circle of fourths and fifths, and this is the design used in this method. Many of the approaches to playing and musical examples given will be relevant, regardless of the style of soprano pan.

Steelpans also tend to vary in terms of range; the examples in this book are specifically catered to soprano pans that have C4 (middle C) as the lowest pitch.

STEELPAN NOTE CHART

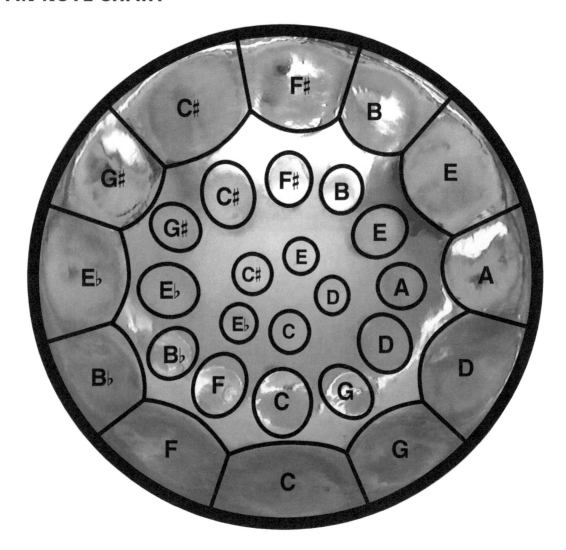

ABOUT THE AUDIO

To access the audio examples that accompany this book, simply go to **www.halleonard.com/mylibrary** and enter the code found on page 1. The examples that include audio are marked with an icon throughout the book.

ABOUT THE AUTHOR

Hailed as the "Paganini of the Steelpan," Liam Teague currently serves as the Head of Steelpan Studies and Associate Professor of Music at Northern Illinois University. Along with Clifford Alexis, he co-directs the NIU Steelband.

He has received many awards in his homeland of Trinidad and Tobago, including the Humming Bird Award (Silver) for "loyal and devoted service" and the Ansa McAl Caribbean Awards for Excellence. Liam has also won of a number of notable competitions, such as the Trinidad and Tobago National Steelband Festival Solo Championship and the Saint Louis Symphony Volunteers Association Young Artiste Competition.

His commitment to demonstrating the great musical possibilities of the steelpan has taken Teague to Europe, Asia, and Australia, as well as North and Central America and the Caribbean. He has performed with many diverse ensembles, including Taiwan National Symphony, Czech National Symphony, Saint Louis Symphony, Panama National Symphony, Chicago Sinfonietta, Vermeer String Quartet, Dartmouth Wind Ensemble, University of Wisconsin-Madison Marching Band, Nexus, TCL Group Skiffle Bunch Steel Orchestra, BPtt Renegades Steelband, and Starlift Steel Orchestra.

Teague has collaborated with such prominent musicians as Paquito D'Rivera, Dave Samuels, Zakir Hussain, and Evelyn Glennie. As a performer and clinician, Teague has given presentations at several Percussive Arts Society International Conventions (PASIC) and at many educational institutions throughout the world.

He is steelband director at Birch Creek Music Performance Center in Door County, Wisconsin, and has also taught and performed at the California State University Summer Arts Camp and the Interlochen Academy for the Performing Arts.

A strong advocate for original steelpan compositions, Teague has commissioned a number of significant composers to write for the instrument, including Michael Colgrass, Jan Bach, Libby Larsen, Deborah Fisher Teason, Joey Sellers, Ben Wahlund, Erik Ross, and Kevin Bobo.

Teague has served as musical arranger of the TCL Group Skiffle Bunch Steel Orchestra, Starlift Steel Orchestra, for Panorama, the most prestigious steelband competition in the world. He is now the arranger for PCS Nitrogen Silver Stars Steel Orchestra.

To date, Teague has recorded eight compact discs, including *Hands Like Lightning* (1993), *For Lack of Better Words* (2002), *Panoramic: Rhythm Through an Unobstructed View* (2005), and *Open Window* (2010).

ACKNOWLEDGMENTS

Dedicated to the people of Trinidad and Tobago, my family, friends, and supporters.

BRIEF HISTORY OF THE STEELPAN

The steelpan (or "pan") is the national instrument of the Republic of Trinidad and Tobago, and represents one of the youngest and most unique families of acoustic instruments created in the 20th century. Initially employed in the late 1930s and early 1940s to provide rhythmic accompaniment for such festive celebrations as Carnival and Christmas, the steelpan has developed in the ensuing decades into one of the most beautiful and versatile instruments in the world.

Its evolution can be traced to enslaved inhabitants of Trinidad and Tobago who were brought to the islands from Africa, primarily to labor on sugar plantations. In 1797, Trinidad became a British colony, in which these enslaved Africans were stripped of freedom and dignity, lost their families, and lived in horrible conditions. These oppressed but resilient people still managed to preserve much of their cultural identity—an essential part of which was drumming, as this played an important role in both their secular and religious traditions.

The colonial masters lived in constant fear that their slaves would revolt, and felt that drumming played an influential part in spreading messages that could insight rebellion. As a result, measures designed to maintain control and dominance were implemented. Such actions took many forms, all intended to promote the superiority of European culture and values, while simultaneously devaluing and suppressing indigenous Trinidadian practices. Often associated with aspects of Carnival celebration, which the British deemed to be vulgar and offensive, hand drumming was eventually banned. Such restrictions would historically be met with strong resistance, which resulted in the rise of alternative forms of cultural expression, including tamboo bamboo ensembles and metal bands.

The tamboo bamboo ensembles consisted of bamboo rods of various lengths and sizes, which were struck together or stomped on the ground to provide rhythm during times of festivity. These instruments gradually disappeared, both due to their lack of durability and use in brutal stick-fighting competitions that the British wanted to end. In their place, metal bands comprised of garbage cans, brake drums, biscuit tins, and caustic soda drums became the music of the day.

The first melodic steelpans evolved from these metal bands. Due to constant striking of the metal drum surfaces during Carnival festivities, the pitches began to change and multiply. These deviations piqued the interest of those who would create the modern steelpan—young men of African descent, the majority of whom hailed from the marginally employed and unemployed sectors of society. The pan's pioneers, though not trained formally in music or science, were deeply engaged in exploring the pitch potential of these instruments by the 1940s. This heralded the birth of the diatonic steelpan. Subsequent trial and error investigation resulted in the chromatic steelpan, enabling musicians to perform a wide range of musical styles including folk songs, calypsos, boleros, and eventually classical music.

Many initially considered the steelpan a mere novelty. They often were skeptical, dismissive, and even abusive to members of the steelpan community. These views were rooted in fear, discrimination, and prejudice that existed on various levels regarding the direct or indirect association of many early steelpan musicians and gangs. Central to the vision of most in the steelpan world, however, was music, the progressive development of the instrument, and its eventual acceptance as a legitimate art form.

Due to the faith, persistence, and sacrifices of these pioneers, bolstered by influential supporters in the middle and upper classes of Trinbagonian society, the pan would eventually captivate the minds, hearts, and souls of the people in its place of birth and around the globe.

STEELPAN ANATOMY

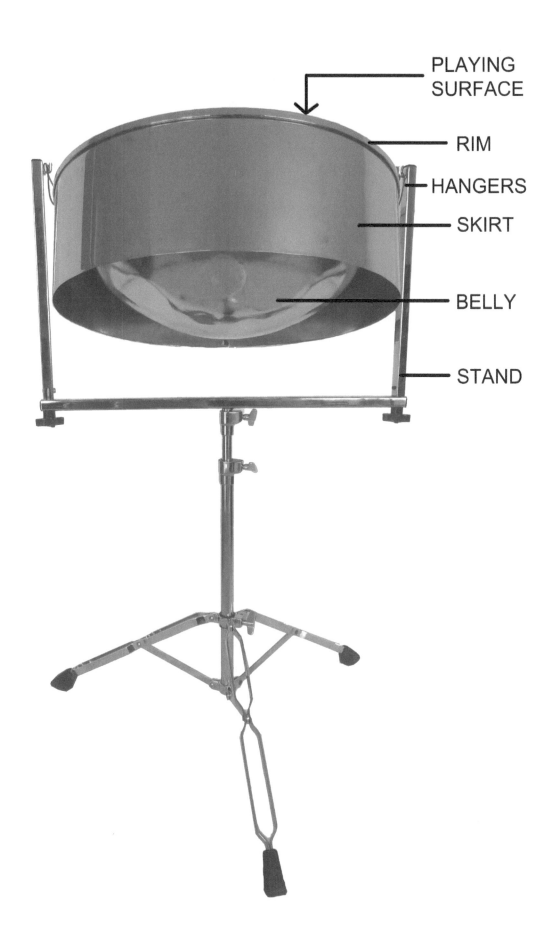

PLAYING SURFACE

RIM

HANGERS

SKIRT

BELLY

STAND

STICKS

Traditionally, steelpan players have used wooden sticks/mallets of various lengths and thicknesses with rubber tips. Nowadays, it has become increasingly popular to play with aluminum shafts. The decision on which to use is a personal choice, however, be sure that the soprano pan mallets are not longer than 6–8 inches. The thickness of the rubber tips should allow the low and high pitches to be heard clearly.

TIPS AND MAINTENANCE

1. Always play and treat the instrument with sensitivity. Do not allow others to get overzealous and bang it out of tune.

2. Keep the instrument out of extreme temperatures. Do not expose the pan to direct sunlight, rain, or cold temperatures as this can compromise the integrity of the metal.

3. Purchase a proper steelpan case. At no point should anything be allowed to strike the underbelly of the instrument. Be sure the case is padded with sponge to protect the instrument from anything that may potentially affect its tuning, however, do not pad the case too tight against the belly of the pan. When traveling, be sure to place "fragile" stickers on the steelpan case.

4. Always try to keep your instrument in a case when it is not being played; however, if you are unable to do so immediately, at least place it cautiously face down on a level surface. Do not set it on the ground on its skirt, as it can easily roll away.

5. Check the hangers on the sides of the steelpan as these can become worn over time.

6. Wipe away any moisture to avoid rusting.

7. Use chrome polish on chromed pans to maintain a brilliant look.

8. Do not place any objects in the pan other than your pan mallets.

9. Do not attempt to tune or repair the instrument yourself. **Be sure to contact an experienced steelpan tuner.**

TECHNIQUE

STANCE

The skirt of the steelpan acts as a resonator, so it needs to be free from any body contact, as doing so will dampen the tonal quality of the instrument. Stand a few inches away from the steelpan and distribute your body weight evenly between both feet.

Generally, it is advisable to be positioned towards the middle of the pan.

However, occasions will arise where shifting one's body, ever so slightly to the left or right, may allow for easier execution.

If necessary, a slight bend of the back or a lean into the instrument can make playing some passages more comfortable.

Be sure to keep your elbows slightly away from your body. Never allow your mallets to drift too far away from the playing surface of the instrument, as this will negatively impact the speed and accuracy of your playing.

HOLDING THE MALLETS

A controlled grip that minimizes the possibility of the sticks/mallets slipping, yet allows for a certain amount of flexibility when notes are struck, is ideal. Sticks should be held between the thumb, first joint of the index finger, and second joint of middle finger of each hand. The ring finger and pinky can be curved around the bottom of the stick or into the palm.

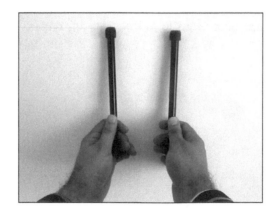

While it is important to maintain a relaxed grip, at times, the sticks may need to be held tighter in order to elicit more volume from some notes. This is especially true with the highest notes on the instrument.

The sticks are normally held as follows:

Palms Down

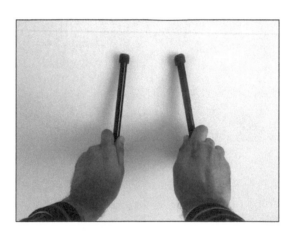

Palms Facing

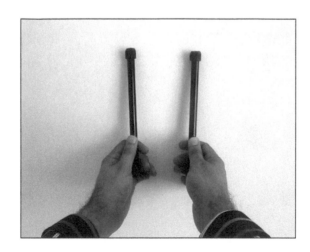

HEIGHT OF STEELPAN STAND

Set the steelpan stand at a height that allows for smooth and comfortable playing. Proper use of the wrists and fingers is essential to good pan technique. Be sure to keep the shoulders and elbows low, so there is no use of the forearms. Music at quick tempos will fatigue a player who uses too much arm.

TYPES OF STROKES

The selection of a stroke type is usually based on the location of the notes in the passage and what feels most physically comfortable. For soprano pan playing, here are the two most frequently applied strokes:

1. Down and up motion: the wrist is bent so as to allow the mallet to strike the note and is instantly returned to the original starting position.

This stroke is normally reserved for notes that are located at the top or bottom of the pan, and either the palms down or palms facing each other grip may be used.

2. Bending of the wrist from left to right or right to left would be most applicable to playing notes located on the side of the instrument. A grip with the palms facing each other would be the most effective one to use.

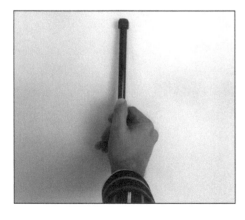 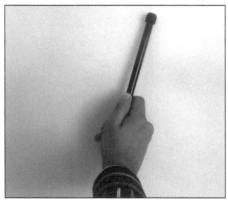 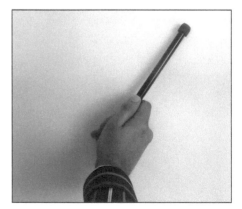

TONE PRODUCTION AND VOLUME CONTROL

Each pitch that you hear in music is made up of a *harmonic series* of several different tones. The *fundamental* is the lowest tone of the series, and typically the pitch that our ears perceive most strongly. To elicit a pure and rich sound from each note on the steelpan, it is important to strike towards the middle of each pitch, or as close to the middle as one can get. This is where the fundamental (or "sweet spot," as it is often referred to in the Caribbean) is located. The sounds that emanate around the edges of the notes will usually either be *harmonics* (the individual, pure tones above the fundamental that make up the harmonic series) or "dead spots" that don't produce an adequate sound. Steelpan note sizes vary, and it can be very easy to miss or "ghost" notes when playing (especially the smaller-sized ones). To minimize the possibility of this happening, one should practice striking the middle of each note at a slow pace for accuracy and then gradually increase the tempo.

The steelpan is an extremely beautiful instrument, but can also sound unpleasant if played too loudly. To minimize this possibility, it is very important to understand your instrument's character. Each pan is unique and some are more resistant to louder playing than others.

A pleasant and consistent tone can be achieved by striking the note from a close distance with the wrists and fingers rather than the arm. Slow, soft practice should be the first step. Gradually, the tempo can be increased but the dynamic should remain soft until you arrive at your goal tempo. The volume can then increase by raising the height of the sticks, increasing the stroke speed, or gripping the sticks tighter. Maintaining a good tone at this volume is still very important. This approach allows the player to maintain dynamic control over the instrument, regardless of tempo, and keeps the instrument in tune much longer.

STICKING

To facilitate smooth playing, it is important to make good sticking choices. Sticking designations are often indicated under notes as: R= Right hand, L= Left hand.

It is generally a good idea to alternate between the right and left hand when striking the notes (R L R L or L R L R), however, instances will arise where this may not produce the best results. On such occasions, doubling the right hand (RR) or left hand (LL) may be more effective. Too many strokes in succession with one hand should be avoided as this can sometimes lead to fatigue and poor tone quality. Over time and with experience, sticking choices will become more intuitive.

NOTE: The suggested stickings in this method may often have several alternatives. Feel free to experiment with different permutations as you become more experienced and confident.

BASIC MUSICAL SYMBOLS

Before you get started with the playing examples, here is a very brief overview of basic music notation.

Staff

Music is notated on a **staff**, which consists of five horizontal lines and four spaces. The highness or lowness (**pitch**) of a note is determined by where it is placed on the staff.

Clef

At the beginning of the staff is a **clef sign**. For the soprano pan, the **treble clef** is used.

Lines

Each of the five notes on the lines of the staff is assigned a letter name. These are, from bottom (low) to top (high): E–G–B–D–F. A helpful way to remember the names of the lines is to think of the phrase "**E**very **G**ood **B**oy **D**oes **F**ine."

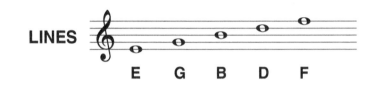

Spaces

The spaces are (low to high) F–A–C–E, which spells "face."

Ledger Lines

To accommodate notes that extend beyond the range of the five-line staff, **ledger lines** are added. In the case of the soprano pan covered in this book, only the lowest note (C) uses a ledger line, just below the staff.

Measures and Bar Lines

To divide the staff into several parts, **bar lines** are used. Bar lines organize counts or **beats** (the steady pulse of music) into groups. The space between two bar lines is called a **measure** (also known as a "bar") and each measure contains a group of beats.

To signal the end of a section of music, a **double bar line** is placed on the staff, and the end of a composition is indicated by a **final bar line**.

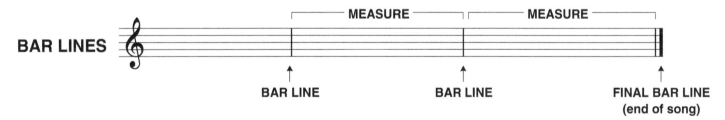

Time Signatures

The number of beats in a measure and the note value that would receive one beat is indicated at the beginning of the staff by a **time signature**. The top number indicates the number of beats in a measure. The bottom number indicates the type of note one beat will receive. **4/4 time** is the most common, in which there are four beats in a measure and a quarter note gets one beat (you'll learn more about note values later).

FIRST NOTES

Get acquainted with your steelpan by playing these first five exercises. Strive for an even tone and steady rhythm. Listen to the accompanying audio tracks to hear how they should sound.

Two-Note Exercise

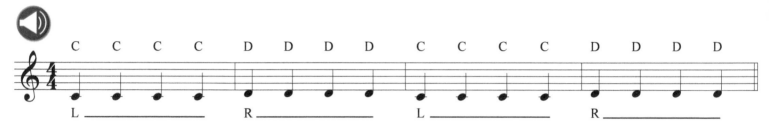

Three-Note Exercise

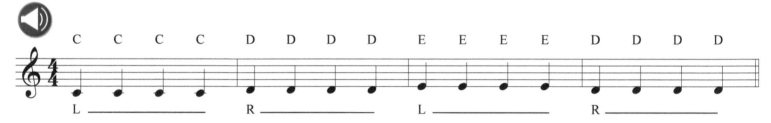

Four-Note Exercise

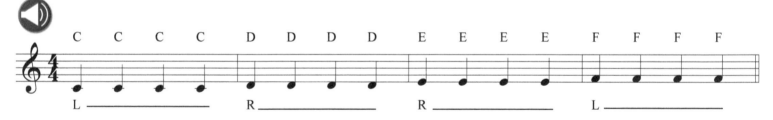

Five-Note Exercise

Where Are They?

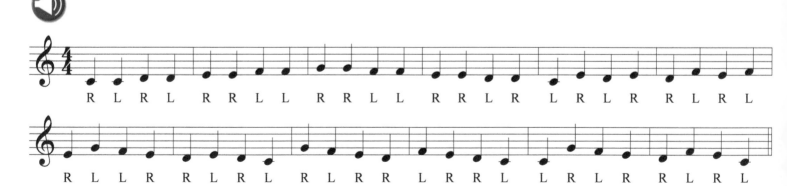

RHYTHMIC VALUES

The **rhythmic value**, or **duration**, of a musical tone is determined by different types of notes within a measure.

𝅝 Whole Note   =   4 beats (or one full measure in 4/4 meter)

𝅗𝅥 Half Note   =   2 beats (or 1/2 measure in 4/4 meter)

𝅘𝅥 Quarter Note   =   1 beat (or 1/4 measure in 4/4 meter)

𝅘𝅥𝅮 Eighth Note   =   1/2 of a beat (or 1/8 measure in 4/4 meter)

𝅘𝅥𝅯 Sixteenth Note   =   1/4 quarter of a beat (or 1/16 of a measure in 4/4 meter)

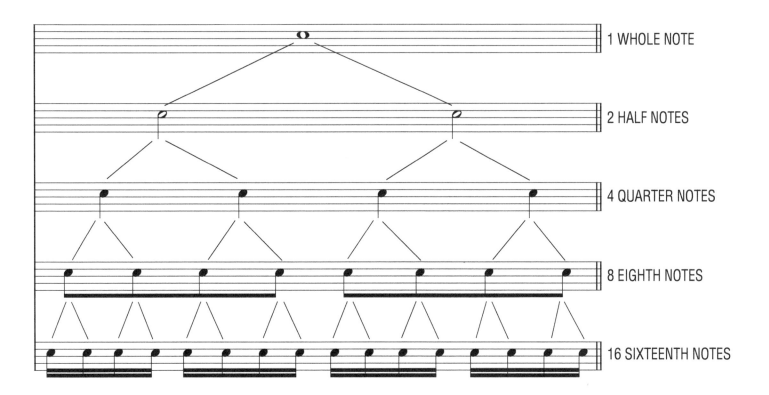

RESTS

A **rest** is a musical symbol that indicates silence. Just like notes, the length of a rest can be measured, and each type of note has a corresponding rest of the same name and duration.

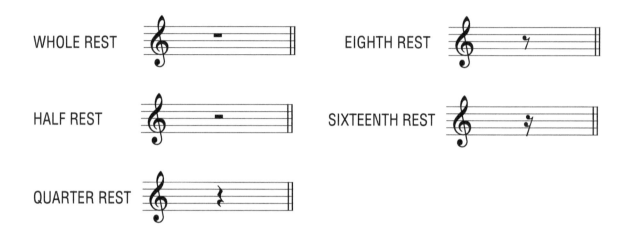

Here's a playing example of a well-known melody that includes rests.

MARY HAD A LITTLE LAMB

Traditional

ROLLS

To achieve a sustained sound on the steelpan, you must roll. A **roll** is produced by quickly and evenly moving the hands in an alternating fashion (right followed by left, or left followed by right) towards the center of a note.

This skill takes time to develop, so start by alternating your hands very slowly and gradually getting faster. Be sure to keep the hands close together without allowing the sticks to rise too far from the playing surface of the pan.

On many occasions, the roll will appear as three short, slanting marks on the stem of a note, however, there are instances when the note(s) to be sustained may be indicated at the beginning of a piece of music in the following manner: "roll quarter note and longer, roll half note, etc."

Rolling Exercise

Play and practice the following tunes that include rolls. Also watch for the eighth notes (more about these later). Listen to the audio track to hear how it sounds.

ODE TO JOY

Ludwig van Beethoven

Here is another well-known melody played with rolls. This tune features a new note, A. Refer back to the steelpan note chart at the start of the book if you need help locating the note A.

TWINKLE, TWINKLE LITTLE STAR
(SIX-NOTE MELODY)

Traditional

The following examples include eighth notes. Remember that these last for half the duration of quarter notes. Listen to the audio tracks to get a feel for this rhythm.

Eighth-Note Exercise

Count: 1 & 2 & 3 & 4 & etc...

FRÈRE JACQUES
(ARE YOU SLEEPING?)

Traditional

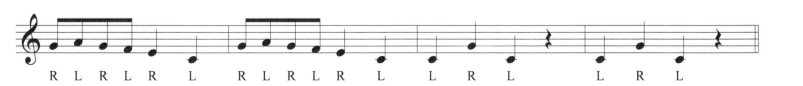

SHORTENIN' BREAD
(SIX-NOTE MELODY)

Folk Song

roll half notes

L R L R L R L R L R L R L R

L L R R L L R L L R R L L R L L R R L L R L R L

JADEN'S SONG
(SEVEN-NOTE MELODY)

roll half notes

L L R L R L R R L L R R

L R L R L R R L R L

SCALES

The distance between music tones, called an **interval**, is measured by **half steps** (H) and **whole steps** (W). A half step is the distance between one "white" note of the piano and the "black" note adjacent to it in either direction. There are also instances of half steps on the piano when two white notes are adjacent to each other without a black note in between them.

A whole step is the distance between two white notes or two black notes. A whole step is equal to two half steps. Taking this idea further, a **scale** is a series of ascending and descending pitches arranged in a specific pattern of whole and half steps.

MAJOR SCALE

A **major scale** is created when the pitches are in this specific pattern: W W H W W W H. Now try the C major scale, which contains all of the notes you have learned so far, plus the higher C note at the top of the scale, an **octave** (same letter name, eight notes away) higher than the **root note** C you already know.

C Major Scale

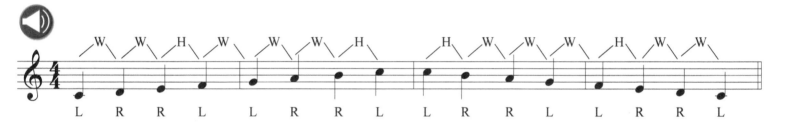

ACCIDENTALS

An **accidental** is a symbol used to alter a note. Specifically, they are **flats**, **sharps**, and **natural signs**.

To lower a pitch by a half step, the flat symbol (♭) is placed before a note. To raise a pitch by a half step, a sharp symbol (♯) is placed before a note.

A natural sign (♮) is used to cancel a flat or sharp from either a preceding note or the key signature (more on key signatures in the following section).

Flats

Sharps

KEY SIGNATURE

The **key signature** is a collection of sharps or flats located between the clef and the time signature at the beginning of a piece of music. It identifies which notes should be raised or lowered throughout the piece to achieve the intended scale and tonal center. If any notes deviate from the key signature, then sharps, flats, and natural symbols are used to alter those notes within the piece.

Next is the F major scale. Notice the key signature that shows one flat symbol on the B line of the staff. This means every B note in the music should be B♭. This scale also includes several new notes that are an octave higher than some of the notes you've already learned.

F Major Scale

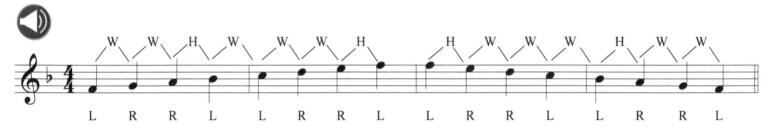

JEIDA'S JUMP

roll half notes

The key signature for the G major scale includes one sharp on the F line. This means every F note in the music should be F#.

G Major Scale

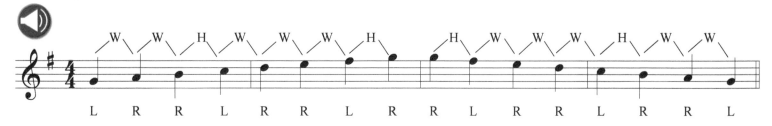

CHICACHANGA

Next try "Ode to Joy" again, but this time in the key of G.

ODE TO JOY

Ludwig van Beethoven

3/4 TIME

The pieces studied so far have all been in 4/4 time (four beats per measure). Let's look at some compositions in **3/4 time** (three beats per measure).

WALTZ FOR CELIA

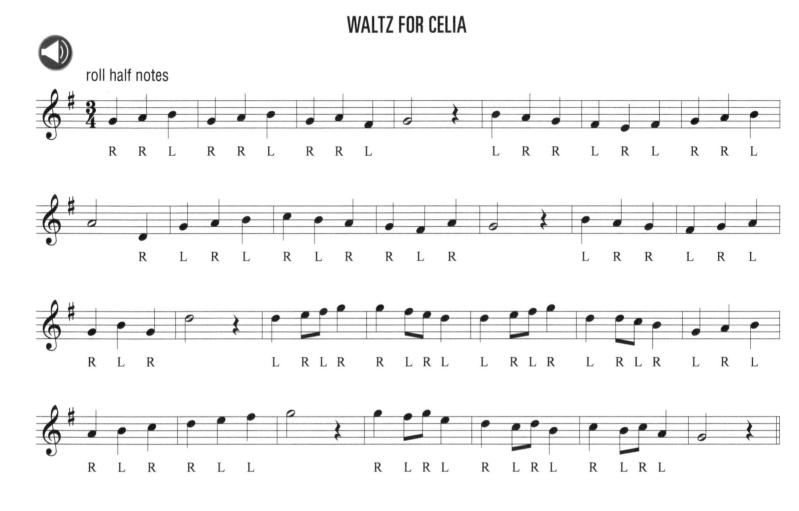

DOTTED NOTES

The **dot** after a note increases its duration by half of its original value. A dotted quarter note would be interpreted as a quarter note plus an eighth note. A dotted half note would be a half note plus a quarter note. Check out the following exercises to get a feel for dotted notes and listen to the audio tracks to hear how they should sound.

Dotted Notes Exercise

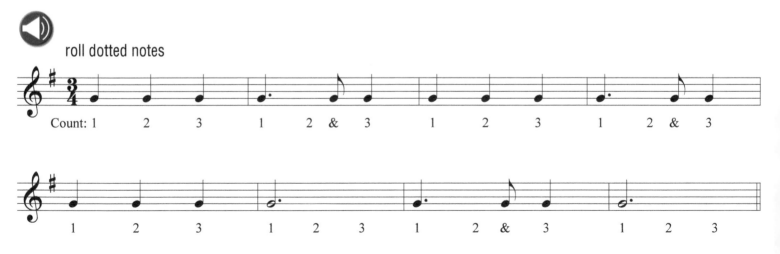

DOT TO DOT

roll dotted notes

Above the next song is a note that indicates you should "roll quarter notes and longer," which means any note that is a quarter note or longer in duration should be rolled.

AMAZING GRACE

Traditional American Melody

roll quarter notes and longer

"Minuet in G" contains a new note, C#.

MINUET IN G

J.S. Bach

roll half notes and longer

CALYPSO

Calypso, like the steelpan, originated in Trinidad and Tobago and is the style of music most commonly associated with steelpans. This music can be instrumental or vocal and examples of great Calypsonians are Lord Kitchener (Aldwyn Roberts), Mighty Sparrow (Slinger Francisco), and David Rudder.

Most calypsos have a heavy presence of **syncopation**, which is the placement of rhythmic accents on weak beats in the measure. A weak beat could be described as the "ands" you say in between each number while counting out the beats of a measure. A number of the musical examples that follow will be relatively simple calypsos.

Before moving on, check out the D major scale, which is used in the calypso songs that follow. This key contains the notes C♯ and F♯, as seen in the key signature.

D Major Scale

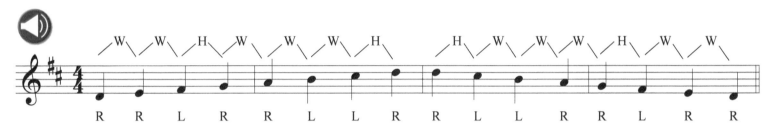

Here are a few rhythms that frequently occur in the calypso style, featuring syncopation:

Calypso Rhythms

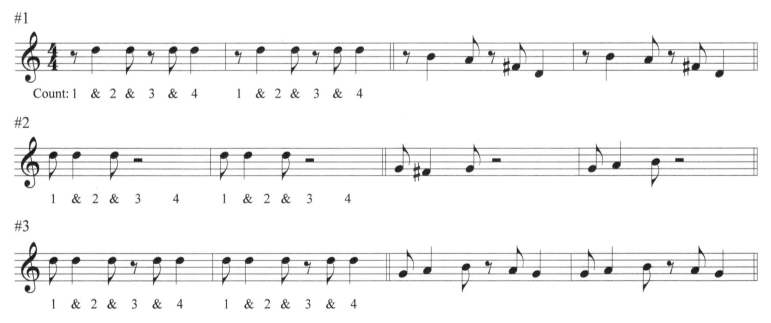

MARY ANN

Rafael de Leon
(a.k.a. "Roaring Lion")

BROWN SKIN GAL

Norman Span
(a.k.a. "King Radio")

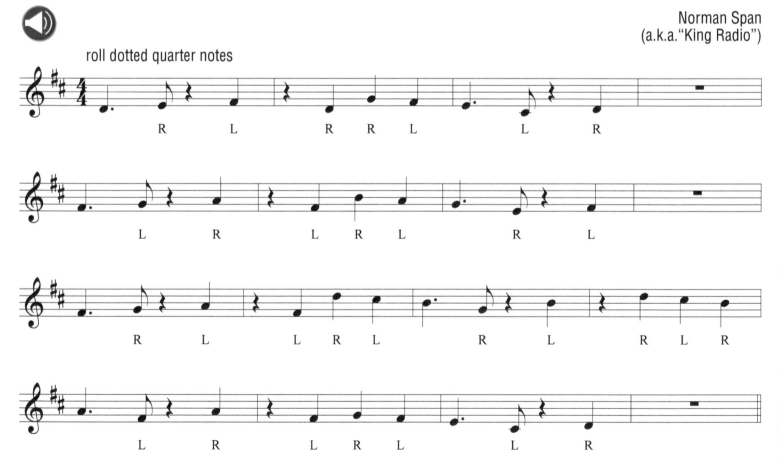

CALYPSO FOR KITCH

LORENA'S CALYPSO

MORE SCALES

The B♭ major scale contains two flats in the key signature: B♭ and E♭.

B♭ Major Scale

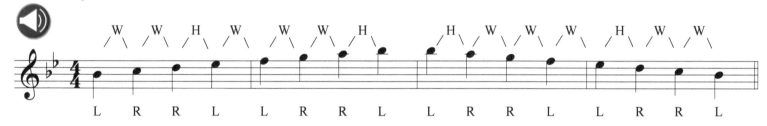

B♭ LEAP

BEE FLAT

MINOR SCALES

In addition to major scales, there are also **minor scales**. Minor scales are made up of a different pattern of whole and half steps. There are three types of minor scales:

Natural Minor: W H W W H W W
A natural minor: A B C D E F G A

Harmonic Minor: same as natural minor except that the seventh note is raised by a half step
A harmonic minor: A B C D E F **G♯** A

Melodic Minor: same as natural minor for notes 1–5, both ascending and descending. On the ascent, raise the sixth and seventh notes by a half step (this will look and sound just like the major scale). On the descent, return to the natural minor scale (lower what was just raised).

A melodic minor (ascending) = A B C D E **F♯ G♯** A
A melodic minor (descending)= A **G F** E D C B A

A Natural Minor

A Harmonic Minor

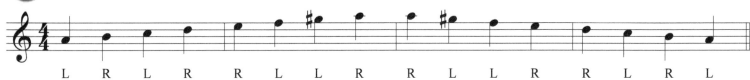

L   L   R   L   R   R   L   L   R   R   L   L   R   R   L   R   L

A Melodic Minor

A melodic minor scale (ascending)

L   L   R   L   R   R   L   L   R

A melodic minor scale (descending)

L   L   R   L   R   R   L   R   L

TRISTE

R   L   R   R   L   R   L   R   L   L   R   L   R   R   L   R   R   L   R   L   L   R

R   L   R   R   L   R   R   R   L   R   L   R   L   R   L   R   L   R   L

R   R   L   R   R   R   L   R   L   R   L   R   L   L   L   R   L   R   R   R   L   R   R

CHROMATIC SCALE

The **chromatic scale** is made up of 12 notes, each a half step apart. Here are examples of ascending and descending chromatic scales starting from the note C.

C chromatic scale (ascending): C C♯ D D♯ E F F♯ G G♯ A A♯ B C

C chromatic scale (descending): C B B♭ A A♭ G G♭ F E E♭ D D♭ C

Notice there are sharps used on the ascending chromatic scale and flats used on the descending version. These sharped and flatted notes are actually the same *sounding* notes; they are simply "spelled" differently, and are called **enharmonic notes**. For example, F♯ is the same note as G♭, just written differently. Why is this done? There are several reasons, but in formal music notation, sharps are often used in ascending musical phrases, while flats are used for descending, as is the case here.

Chromatic Scale Exercise

roll half notes and longer

C chromatic scale (ascending)

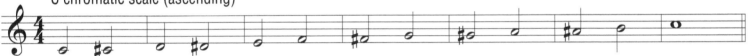

C chromatic scale (descending)

The final piece is in a calypso style and features the key of B♭ major along with several chromatic notes. Enjoy!

LAGNIAPPE